T0355991

libre

"With *libre*, Skye Jackson gifts us with a complicated, intimate and searingly honest love letter to New Orleans, to family, and to the embodied tenderness of black feminine being within—and crucially: despite—America. Jackson depicts unflinching but compassionate portraits of sibling suicide and the strange, continuous grief that accompanies it; the messiness of interracial love and its resultant interrogations between self and other; and radically reconsiders Western art via ekphrastic self-insertion ('#medusawasblackyall'). These poems are sung conversationally, with a generosity of voice that wraps the reader in both their warmth and horror, as in Jackson's elegy for Kori Gauthier: 'i was like you once. saw the river as comfort, a dark crib, to nurse my suffering. the water, stygian & full of possibilities, delicious silence.' Their casual whimsy often belies a delicious, bitter eye for irony, but also veers so frequently, so precipitously, towards a novel rearticulation of the interior terror that microaggressions so often inflict upon our blackness. Jackson's ingeniously titled poem 'far too kind' perhaps best exemplifies this: in which she can never forget (or forgive) the gaze of racism, where she is 'still aware of that stare // that followed me / to the dining room table / that passed me the coq au vin / that poured another rush of bourgogne into my glass / that crushed me / with polite conversation.'"

—Tawanda Mulalu, *Nearness* and *Please make me pretty,
I don't want to die: Poems*

"Skye Jackson's debut collection marked with one word, libre, is so full while extending an intimate invitation to all of us to explore: How do we enter the state of our own sense of freedom? With each poem and each page, the collection pierces in all the ways good verse does. *libre* pierces the veil between living and dead whether we see Jackson's poetry present the truth about the equalizing power of the cemetery to a fever dream to the ways that ghosts of the once living never leave us. *libre* penetrates the gates that stand between us and what we know as self-emancipation in intimate scenes that weave love, family, memory, and the required Tetris of navigating skin inheritance. *libre* brings us into a depth of intimacy that vanishes the boundaries of our very human lives and the nature that surrounds us whether it is wasps in the mailbox to the way snow can write a love letter to a boy. The collection is bookcased by two encounters. One that opens the collection and ends with a socio-cultural-historical dismemberment. And the last poem that speaks that kind of fierce declaration of self-pointing to what we need to understand about our own state of free breaking through the membrane of what we might have forgotten with a reminder. A reminder to embrace a reclamation that we keep as the lullaby that we whisper into our own ears."

—**Shanta Lee**, *Black Metamorphoses* and *This Is How They Teach You How to Want It…The Slaughter*

i ask myself: where do you run when nowhere, not even home, will suffice?

Skye Jackson's moving poems trace the journeys of a young Black woman dealing with issues of family, death, dating, and the daily work of navigating micro- and macro-aggressions, and casual racism, in a world where gentrification is 'another word//for *revenge*.' Set in various locations—Paris, Vermont, Key West—but always returning to her native New Orleans, Jackson limns the joys and obstacles of being an object of desire while also attempting to develop into your own person. *libre* unerringly depicts the process of building a self from the disparate elements of life

out of the wild thick
a shape takes place
kind of like
this poem

—**Reginald Harris**, *Autogeography*

"'The defenseless are still defenseless/ no matter where you go,' writes Skye Jackson in her raw, musical, and imagistically rich, *libre*. In this collection, we are caught between fever and dream, between the warped realities of racialized violence and the emotional realities that adjust our inner worlds forever. Objects speak and move the fates: black mold, sugar, a dead tree, a porcelain spoon rest, a blue fiat, mussels, a paper carnation. There is no inanimate 'thing' in this book; every object has agency, history, can be weaponized or used for comfort. Jackson masterfully orchestrates destinies that are pieced and dismembered before our eyes. Some 'burst like a supernova' and others remain 'defenseless' yet in Jackson's language, even those without protection have an archive, a voice, or find forms."

—**Meg Fernandes,** *I Do Everything I'm Told* **and** *Good Boys: Poems*

LIBRE

SKYE JACKSON

A REGALO PRESS BOOK

Libre
© 2025 by Skye Jackson
All Rights Reserved

ISBN: 979-8-88845-478-7
ISBN (eBook): 979-8-88845-479-4

Cover design by Jim Villaflores
Cover photo by Benjamin Aleshire
Interior design and composition by Greg Johnson, Textbook Perfect

PUBLISHING TEAM
Founder and Publisher: Gretchen Young
Editor: Caitlyn Limbaugh
Managing Editor: Aleigha Koss
Production Manager: Alana Mills
Production Editor: Rachel Paul
Associate Production Manager: Kate Harris

This book, as well as any other Regalo Press publications, may be purchased in bulk quantities at a special discounted rate. Contact orders@regalopress.com for more information.

As part of the mission of Regalo Press, a donation is being made to One Book One New Orleans, as chosen by the author. Learn more about this organization at https://onebookonenola.org/.

This is a work of nonfiction. All people, locations, events, and situations are portrayed to the best of the author's memory.

Regalo Press
New York • Nashville
regalopress.com

Published in the United States of America
1 2 3 4 5 6 7 8 9 10

Contents

can we touch your hair?

at the parades, everyone
wants to touch my hair.

on the corner
of st. charles and marengo,

i am cold & smashed & puffy AF
when two white women
try to convince me
that they love my hair

no they *really really* do
they say because it is so
black and thick and curly
and soaking up all of the
water in the damp air.

the mousy one says
through an alabama drawl:
gawd, you can do so much with it

and her blonde friend says:
ya can't do a damn thing with mine,
won't even hold a curl.

she runs away to grab another friend
and says to her: *stacey, isn't it even*
prettier than macy gray's?
we just love her
don't we?

they circle me
& ask:
can we touch your hair?

then suddenly
just like my ancestors long ago,
i am pulled apart

soft

by pale hands
from all directions.

blackbirds singing in the dead

last night outside my window
i heard a family of blackbirds
cry restless in a paper nest

then the little boy knocked
on my bedroom door he
heard our dead brother
moving 'round the attic again

i wonder
is 'los ready for someone
to cut him down

dead brother
how dare you
sway there
just so

little boy,
don't take his hand

let the rope burn
around his neck
remind you
that he is no longer
of this world

there it goes
there it goes (again)
says the little boy
i swear he's up there
i swear he's calling
out my name

i almost answered too
heard him kick out
the chair from beneath
his own feet

then the little boy
looked at me,
his long brown fingers
trembling
& said:

dad didn't even know what his
favorite song was skye do you
think he knows mine skye do
you think he hears mine skye

i remember

do you hear that?

it's the sound of a white girl
on a blue bike riding up st. claude
on her way down to st. bernard

it's the sound of a european wax center
newly built on freret st.
it's the sound of the last
mom & pop coffee shop
being torn down on the westbank
& a starbucks going up
in its place

it's the sound of my mama's voice
as she taps on the window glass
when we drive down burgundy
she points to a renovated row
of candy-colored shotgun houses
and says:
i remember
when only black people
lived over here

it's the sound of my cousin saying:
i remember
when it was easy to buy
a starter house in gentilly

or my boyfriend being illegally evicted
because airbnb needs
more room for tourists
in the crescent city

it's the sound of my best friend
buying a house
all the way out in kenner
because he and his wife
can no longer afford
to live in orleans parish

i close my eyes
& when i open them
lorraine hansberry stands before me
glowing brown, like our virgin mary

in one palm, she holds a raisin
& in the other, revolves a sun

she whispers to me:
i remember when they wouldn't let us in
& now they're pushing us out

& in my mind—
a chilling realization:
gentrification is just
another word
for *revenge*

let's call it what it is:
allow the snake squeezing us dead
to shed its skin

get ray nagin on the prison phone
let him know that this chocolate city
has officially melted

the little gray schnauzer

—after elizabeth bishop

still waits in the empty kitchen.
his silver head tilts
against a wave of fringe on the rug
beneath the long-cooled stove,
as though he expects
that at any moment,
my mother will walk in
with a bundle of lemons
picked from the tree in the backyard,
set her gatherings down,
stir brown sugar & cream together
to make pralines;
or that my father's loafered heels
will clack briskly along the hardwood floor,
prompt from the grocery
to hand her the butter she needs;
or that my brother will saunter in,
beautiful & wordless,
the tails of his shearling camel coat
trailing like attendants behind him,
to stick one ringed finger
into the sweet mixture,
reach down to the rug
& give him just one lick.
the little gray schnauzer waits &
i sit down next to him to wait, too.

fever dream

my mama stepped
from fever into dream
one night:

wished for my great-grandmother
and found herself standing
in front of her house

said it was exactly
as she remembered it
before katrina, protected
by the pale silver gate too

and when she walked inside,
she saw the mantelpiece
as it stood before the panels
were warped by moisture
and covered
with black mold

she passed
pictures of herself
pigtailed and peter pan collared
frozen in seventies sepia tint
and focused her gaze
on the open doorway
to the kitchen

Mother stood at the stove
and stirred a pot of red beans
when my mama heard her say
sit down, child, & rest some

my mama buried her face
in her small light hands

& the minutes
dripped by
on the old wooden clock
in the hall

she sat in her dead grandmother's
dead kitchen & cried
until she woke up
alone, pillows damp

later, she called me
& said:

skye why didn't i ask her
what i needed to?

how come all i could do
in her presence
was cry?

i just listened
to my mama
because i knew
that's what she needed
instead of the sweet
emptiness
of a daughter's
naïve reply

both hands on the wheel

i think of philando castile's
murder every single summer

& the moment i heard about it
in my hollywood studio,
so hot, even the walls
sweated

on my phone, i watched
as a black man raised
his hands
& lost his life

somehow
the cell phone camera
captured the last breath
fleeing from his body

i thought of my father,
tired, white-collared & necktied,
both hands on the wheel
of the family SUV,
hurtling towards home
down some dark country road

or my little brother
cruising through a bustling city,
tan convertible top down,
the thick wild tufts
of his black hair
dancing in the wind

until he is stopped
by some sunglassed officer
& leaning out of the window
of his blue fiat

code switched, breath clipped
as a millennium slips
between his hand & pocket
to show his ID
to the cop
as he wonders
whether it is safe
or not
to ask:

why did you pull me over, officer?
why did you
pull me
over?

a faster grave

did i tell you that
my daddy just started
a war on sugar?

wanted me to comb
through each kitchen cabinet
& trash all granulated specks.

while you're at it, he said,
throw out that white bread too.
these things are killing us.

but i contemplated a different death
the one i'd meet
if my mama couldn't find
the domino sugar cubes
for her coffee
or the bunny bread
for her turkey sandwiches

keep on listening to your dad,
she clucked,
& i'll dig you a faster grave

the cemetery

my mama & my great aunt
have fought for the last three years
over my great-grandmother's
rebuilt house on gallier street
in the ninth ward

which family members
should get to stay there
& who shouldn't
which family members
should pay the rising
property taxes
& which shouldn't

you should see it over there now, skye,
my mama says,
mostly white people now
they're taking the neighborhood back—
the way it used to be
before all us black folks moved in

my cousins and i stay out of the fight
we talk to each other on the sidelines
like second-string football players
rooted to the bench

over eggplant pirogue at copeland's,
my cousin nicole says:
i see the points each are making
i understand both sides

yesterday, my great aunt
who is now in her late seventies
finally issued a détente

sent my mama a message:
are you going to the cemetery
to see Mother & Lil?
i haven't been since the pandemic started
& i'd like to go

all i can think is that
i suppose it's true what they say:
the cemetery truly does
bring us all
back together
in the end

my dad doesn't know how to fight the wasps in the mailbox

so i give him some advice
like the Kitchen Oracle i am

i google: how to chase wasps
from the mailbox

and search engine overlord
suggests dryer sheets,
or building a fake nest to confuse them,
also a potion of essential oils to spray:
clove, geranium, lemongrass, and rosemary

my dad says:
every week i chase them away
but they still come back

i nod and i joke:
don't you know
we're in a housing crisis
good real estate
is hard to come by

idk he says
i'm just starting
to take this whole thing
personally

i say:
dad, last week
i got drunk at R Bar
and they were playing this footage
of a frog protecting its nest
of tadpoles
on a leaf in the rain forest

the wasps kept trying to steal
the eggs
and the frog kept kicking
and kicking the wasp away
with its long sticky lime legs

and then the wasp got pissed
and ran away to get its friends

                                              blank stare

i say all this to say:

1) wasps are the assholes of the animal world
    so don't take it personally

2) somewhere out there
    there is a frog on a leaf
    in the middle of the rainforest
    who feels *exactly*
    the same way you do

survival:
the only language
all of our tongues
speak

so don't feel alone

does that make you feel better

when i visit my father in the hospital

we talk about everything
except what brought him here

how are you,
i ask him,
not for the real answer
but just to obey some cosmic
formality that i do not understand

i don't want to hear the truth
just as much as he doesn't want
to say it out loud

i tell him about the dog
where i'm housesitting
right off of st. bernard

all the machines he's hooked to
beep so loudly
i can't even hear myself think

i say, *his name is goji*
yesterday he pulled me down in the grass
chasing ducks by the bayou

i tell him about the two cats
the turtle
and the snail
that hasn't moved for days
in its terrarium

it just sticks to the same wall
i say,
idk what it's waiting for

the nurse removes
the emptied hospital plates
& adjusts his bed
it's time to turn you over
she says,
that's why this machine is beeping

finally
it is my dad's turn to speak
slowly, he asks me
if my boyfriend plays the guitar

he tells me
about a funeral he attended
for one of his friends
just the weekend before
he was admitted
to the hospital

the guitarist played a solo
he said, smiling,
it was Amazing Grace

with a light in his eyes, he said,
it was so moving
i wondered how someone could
make you feel so deeply
without even singing
one single word

he said,
i decided then
i'm gonna learn to play the guitar too
and smoothed the blankets
on his hospital bed
when i get out of here
i'll have my first lesson

questions

my professor leaked us a copy of toi derricotte's
book *i* before it was officially released
because she is magic
& apparently money manipulates bookstores.

this light-skinned woman smiling up at me,
awash in gray on the cover
& wrapped in poetic turtleneck,
reminds me of my light-skinned mother.

she married a man with deep skin
and had children darker
than she would ever be.

my mama said: *skye, i wish you'd been born*
with my grandfather's green eyes.
i wonder if your children will have them.

years later, i pick up my white boyfriend from school
because he's broken his arm in that reckless way
that white people are allowed to break things.

he slides into my car with green eyes
reflecting the sunlight and sees toi's book
on the passenger seat.

he tells me that he is introducing her at a reading.
he has questions:

  i   how did you get that book?
      i answer: professorial magic, i suppose.

ii is it toi like toy? toi like an actual toy?
    i answer: pronunciation: yes. spelling: no.

iii babe, is she white?
    i answer: no
    she is black like my mama is black
    just not as brown as me.

far too kind

i walk into the dining room
and sit down
as candles
light up a thicket
of white faces
that surround me

across the table
a lady smiles at me
and says
god i loved your book
it was so real

she talks
as everyone else
prods their slick
mandarin salads
and listens

my mind is still outside
uptown on peniston
and circles the block
in search of
a place to park

i flip my thick twists
out of my eyes
check my teeth
for red lipstick
in the rearview mirror

i find a spot
as a white woman
draped in the shadow
of a dark mansion
across the street
has stopped
to watch
me

her platinum hair shines
white as sin
under the streetlights

her gaze sharp
like an elegant heel
pinned into
the nape of my neck

i lock the car door
turn to her and smile hello
but she doesn't respond—
just stares

as i walk up to the house
fumble with the fence latch
still aware of that stare

that followed me
to the dining room table
that passed me the coq au vin
that poured another rush
of bourgogne into my glass
that crushed me
with polite conversation

my hand shakes slightly
as i finally respond
thank you so much for reading
you are far too kind

spoon rest mammies

i.

on tuesday at work
my manager, a brown latina
married to a black man,
approaches me

with a smile she sets
something down
in front of me
and asks
*what do you think
about these?*

i look down
at a porcelain spoon rest
shaped into the swollen
figure of a mammy:

her lips exaggerated
& face dark
like the trunk of a dead tree

the dress painted jemima red
with a white apron
tied chain-taut
around her waist

my heart races in its cage
after a second i say
*we shouldn't sell these
they are offensive*

my manager purses her lips
sighs and says
but they sell, my dear skye
people buy them

ii.
at the end of my shift
a latina woman
with frizzy bleached blonde
hair stands in front of me:
i'm from california
she says
just buying these for my kids
as a joke

they're gonna be so mad
i bought these

she hands me two
of the mammy spoon rests
& says
make sure you wrap them up good
i'd hate
for them to break
on the flight back home

so i protect them
in paper and bubble wrap
carefully place each one
in a plastic bag
you know, the lady says
your store shouldn't carry these

i hand her the bag
smile and say
but they sell

iii.

three weeks later
my manager
hands me a cardboard box

i open it
to each spoon rest mammy
huddled together

they smile up at me
from the guts of the box

my manager says
i tried to donate them to goodwill
but the guy accepting donations said:
i won't sell these

but if you want
i can throw them
in the dumpster out back

i'd be happy
to do that

ice cream sam

ice cream sam picks me up
down on burgundy;
it's the wednesday
before christmas
when i climb into his truck

his seventh ward accent drips
in my ear like molasses,
sweet & slow

he tells me about his cats
the flavors he creates
& pours his soul into

he names one "butter off dead"
& i love him already
as we arrive at the restaurant
on esplanade, café degas,
all lit up
& yet still dim

i'm the only
black person in the restaurant,
of course

except for our waiter
who seems distant
& does not keep
my glass filled
with wine

ice cream sam orders
the whole menu for us:
mussels, sweet breads, & french onion soup

he sips sparkling water –
gave up the booze & drugs
years ago, you know?

but later,
when we stand
in line to ride
the coaster at city park
& the icy wind
bites our cheeks,
i realize
he still loves
a good rush,
gets giddy
at the thought of it

he puts his big calloused hands
inside the belly
of my fluffy coat

tonight, on that coaster
we'll swirl together
round & round
until we are cold
& sweet
just like his french
gourmet ice cream

umbrella

on just another day
of relentless rain
in new orleans

i studied the girl
planted in front of my register
for a long time;
grey hoodie drenched
her dark eyes
refused my glance
but somehow

the red paper carnation tied
around her wrist
dry as linen
hung on a clothesline

she picked up an umbrella
from a basket on the floor
and walked slowly to the door

i stopped her

as she stood one foot
beyond the threshold
are you gonna pay for that,
i asked trembling

she looked up at me
brown eyes endless
as the earth
her skin deep
chicory like my own

she smiled at me through
closed mouth
& never opened her lips
once to speak

she handed me the umbrella
tucked underneath her arm

the flower on her wrist
opened slightly in the wind

as she walked out
into the slaughter of rain

to my best friend getting married on the sixteenth anniversary of hurricane katrina

forgive me
this past year i laced your veil
with dread
planned your bridal shower
states away through zoom calls
was not there to see your curls bounce
warm in the boutique light
as you picked out
your dress

we are no strangers to disaster
racing through flood waters as children
holding our gowns
up to our knees
just trying to get to prom
on time

waded in dark water
through our drowned city

i leave
as a familiar darkness
looms at the door

i'll watch you walk
down the aisle
your curls veiled
& makeup freshly applied

i'll think of the love
you're racing to
and that bereft city
we've longingly
left behind

no foul play suspected

for kori gauthier

> "Everyone warns us off the rocks. /
> But what will keep us from the river?"
>
> —Eugenia Leigh

you left your phone & purse open on the passenger seat
in a new car on a bridge overlooking the mississippi
river. you did not take the keys out of the ignition. you
left the car, an eighteenth birthday present from your
parents, still running. you rushed to your blind date
with death as though it were the dental appointment
scheduled in your google calendar for the next
morning. there was no need for seduction. you were a
sure thing. you stood on the cement lip of the bridge
and cast yourself over the guardrail without a sound,
like a fishing line, gliding into the muddied water.

your headlights were still on as the tow truck arrived. no
one, not even the tow truck driver, stopped to wonder
why. lights on. car running. phone & purse inside.
engine still breathing, though you were no longer.
when he rigged your car to his truck without so much
of a backward glance, he confirmed your haunting: *no
one cares.* i imagine your ochre eyes: beautiful & sick
with tired, anchored to the water below. tell me this:
if no one is around to hear the sound of a brown girl
plunging like a dagger into a river, did she ever even fall

at all? *no foul play suspected*, is all that the papers will say. *out of respect for the family*, the police chief refuses to speak on the topic any further. they will not call your death a suicide *out of respect*. the drowned girl silenced twice. i ask myself: where do you run when nowhere, not even home, will suffice?

i was like you, once. saw the river as comfort, a dark crib, to nurse my suffering. the water, stygian & full of possibilities, delicious silence. what if i had driven off the bridge, as desire called me to, under the blurred veil of my tears? a wedding of brown water & browner skin. would i have beckoned to you from the river bottom on a jagged marital bed of rock? the current pushing our bodies, together, as the curve of the moon smiled down at the light of its own reflection on the water.

on canal street, i stand in line to be covid tested

when the loctitian
calls to tell me
that it will be $700
to save my brother's hair

years of delicate uncare
have led to this:
a matted forest of thick hair,
unloved & unattended to

as the nurse swabs my nose
i think most of it
is a lost cause
& will need
to come off

my brother asks only
to keep
the long tendril
that hangs in his face
the only part
of his hair
he cannot bear to let go of

i am walking back to the apartment
when i get an email with my results:
positive
as though the fever,
rising slow like an escalator,
weren't already an indication

the next night, in quarantine,
i learn the loctitian
somehow salvaged
all of his hair
it only took about a day—
about eighteen hours in her chair

she shaped his hair
into free form locs

my brother emerged
looking like a baby basquiat
locs sausage thick & full
jutting out from his head
in all directions

out of the wild thick
a shape takes place
kind of like
this poem

which one

"It is very uncommon for young black men
to commit suicide, let alone by hanging."

—Raymond Winbush, *The Washington Post*.
   June 22, 2020

i hid the gun
when my father
asked me to

my little brother
told my parents twice
what he planned
to do

they were alarmed
after all
their oldest son
had chosen
rope instead

his body bent limp
into dangled bloat
the brown skin
around his neck
peeled off into strips

they tell me:
suicides always leave a note

but my older brother
who often wrote
and always drew
somehow forgot
as he tightened
the noose

as i tucked the gun
away in my dresser drawer
and buried it
beneath folded clothes,
like a gift
hidden away
to surprise a friend,

i heard the past echo
of my father's voice
in my head:
your brother's dead
breaking cool like ice
on that warm august night
and i remember
that i couldn't bear
to ask him
which one

[the boys with dead mothers
get better with time]

the boys with dead mothers get better with time. the
white boy in law school eluded me—like a flash of
light in murky water. hid me away in study rooms, or
his parents' mississippi mansion like a letter that wasn't
supposed to be read. or when i asked him about the
book in his car, *the goldfinch*, after we spent the night
together. he told me it was about a boy and a painting.
not a boy and his dead mother. how years later, it would
all make sense. in LA the boy with the dead mother
begged me not to leave him the first night we met. over
louis armstrong and wine he kissed me and just said:
stay. in new orleans, the boy with the dead mother tells
me that he missed his mother's gravy at my parent's
house this past thanksgiving. he asks me if we can roast
a chicken to replicate the thickness of the sauce: the
way she smeared seasoning all over it. he tells me how
he and his father fought over the bacon she laid tender
over the breasts like blankets. why do i love boys whose
mothers are dead? what am i hoping that they see in
me? what am i hoping that they don't?

girl crush sonnet

cheeks flush with blush on a saturday night
her: the only black girl in the bar be-
sides me—typewriter at my side; page boy
hot girl moves towards me, glances exchanged
over the thrum of sound; she is the queen
of slouchy girl vibes, yes. willie nelson
tee stuffed into dark blue jeans. she moves quick
through the electric air & fantasies
swim through the room. heartbeats as she asks me
for my number. wonder where the night will
lead next; *skye, i want to see some tits bounce
tonight*, she whispers. so off to the strip
club we go—except i can't get in; no
cash. her text reads: *come back. i'll cover you.*

an ode to the w paris

i'm in berlin
& you're in barcelona
but the plan is
to meet in paris

and though it has been
only a week since
we've seen each other

i've got half a mind
to greet you in the lobby
of our five-star hotel
on rue meyerbeer

in the ratty shirt
that i sleep in
and the grey sweatpants
you left behind

i'll wait for you
as the bellboy rushes
past and shuffles along
cases of louis vuitton luggage

i'll stand under the fanciest
chandelier i can find
with my braids
hung loose at my sides

so that the first thing
you wonder
is not what we will have
for dinner
in this decadent behemoth

but rather
which is softer:

my lips
or the slip of your hand
down into my pocket
to find
the room key

to comfort you

i want to whisper to you
while you sleep

catch you in that quiet world
between starlight & dawn

with my hand on the crook of your arm
i'll come as close as i can get &
ask you why in the museum today
you saw your father in every black &
white photograph
or as a phantom in paintings

here in paris,
all you can think of
dream of is mid-city
and the art on your walls
how you hope the coming storm
back in new orleans won't claim them
not your house not your bike
not your books but your art

in the art nouveau exhibit,
i stand in an ornate mirror & say:
i want one just like this

you knot your scarred arm in mine
and tell me that the only thing you'll inherit
is a beautiful old looking glass
and there's no one you want to see
reflected in it but me.

so here in the darkness
i butter my black body
in coconut oil & wait for my eyes to adjust.
when they do,
i watch your body slip in and out
of covers and dreams

i want to ask you as you sleep
to just call the old man
even though you won't
even though you can't
because your dreams of him
watching you run through a field of dandelions
when you were a boy
are all you need
to comfort you

currency

in paris, even the violence
is cinematic.
in hot summer,
shoes fly through the sticky air
tables launched like rockets
& blood spattered shirts scream:
witness this revolution.

as i watch in horror
four men tear at one another
the blood on their teeth glistening
like red melted licorice
in the midday sun.

a rush of black skin against black skin
in the most physical war i've ever seen—
up close, that is.

and all this at the entrance of the train
i think, wow this is just like new orleans
and my boyfriend laughs & says, yeah except
there they'd all have guns & right now
the news would spread how
at least eight or more are dead.

my american instinct
forces me to duck and rush
to escape bullets
that won't ever come.

then suddenly,
all the tickets on the train are free
and we pass through the station
with only our lives as currency.

i think of a twilight zone episode
when an alien said:
people are the same everywhere
and i agree
because in paris & new orleans
violence packs its bags
but never takes a vacation.

that episode was right:
the defenseless are still defenseless
no matter where you go.

under the shadow of a golden clock

in musee d'orsay
i wander among the work of berthe;
see her paintings of maids bent
over to wash linens
and a self-portrait of the artist
clad in brown and looking incredibly stern

but downstairs hidden in a corner
underneath the shadow of a golden clock:
an exhibit devoted to black models of the past.
jeanne duval, the mistress of a poet,
high yellow & in recline

and just past her a painting of ira aldridge:
the first *actual* black person
to play othello onstage

though the portrait shows him
shackled and chained,
he still glances up towards the sun

and i think of the moment he recited
his lines to the crowd and alexander dumas
stood up & exclaimed *i am a negro too*
and i whisper the words to myself

i stand hidden in a crowd of people
rushing past me to see *olympia*,
the painting in which manet
captured what appears to be
the first ever recorded side-eye
cast towards a white woman

and no one can see me
but josephine baker
who looks down at me
from an old recording smiling
lips slicked dark breasts bared
knees shimmying
with so much laughter in her eyes

i look up at her and whisper, *sister*
i look up at her and whisper, *friend*

and my boyfriend finds me lost
and says, *i am so full*
are you ready to go?
and i look at him ravenous
because i will never be filled
and i refuse to clear my plate

the women in the wood

cézanne painted *the large bathers*,
eight women in the wood,
the clouds resting behind them
like cotton

each body bare in the twilight
some hold white sheets
or have them nestled
in their laps

i wonder
why he chose to paint them
without mouths:
imagine, a group of women
gathered together
who cannot even speak

their pale bodies under the moonlight
its own language of curve & softness
cheeks ruddied flush
by the warm night

i want this painting remade
with my beautiful brown girlfriends
all of our bodies different shades
mouths actualized
full lips dripping with laughter
& talk of upcoming sins
hairs laid smooth
or rising wild
towards the moonlit sky,
all thickness & soft curl

#medusawasblackyall

—after Benvenuto Cellini, "Perseus with the
    head of Medusa," bronze sculpture

perseus, hold my dead lips
up close to your ear.
let me tell you a secret
with my split tongues.

once, long ago,
poseidon held a fistful
of my black locs
just like this.

on the floor of the temple,
fingers pulling at my scalp,
he inhaled me; my body
soft from lavender and holy oil.

my robes, cast off and torn,
spilled down over the altar
and even the candles
dimmed in respect of my shame;
my brown skin somehow paled
in the fading light.

the last thing i remember
before the snakes came,
before my body was lost
both to the sea and to knowledge:
a reflection of myself,

in the eyes of that cruel god.
the imprint of his hands,
hot and red as the sea on my neck.
the chill of them
first touching my face—

the press and dead fish stink
of that salty mouth,
lips rough and cold
as the jagged rocks of the deep
against my collarbone.

picture a girl built pretty and open
like a temple, only to be destroyed.

be kind: you are looking at ruins
further ruined.

what i mean to say
is that the swift kiss
of your sword on my neck
is not unfamiliar, perseus.

i have tasted the sharp, quick
pain of a man before.

& the truth is

on facebook
i post pictures
of my black self
in a white dress

when an older blonde
white lady comments
not on the words of my post
or my thick dark dreads
or the way the city park sun
caught every gradient
of brown in my cheeks
those red undertones
my mama always said
she could see

no,
she comments
on the necklace
i'm wearing:

a silver feather
dangling across
my collarbone

the one that the white boy
who'd flown in
from los angeles
bought for me in the Quarter
because he *had* to see it
around my neck

how do white people
know their own
so much
that they can spot it
from a picture?

(& the truth is
only a white boy
would want to keep
a feather
trapped
on a chain)

black girl in the backseat

one rainy afternoon
my uber driver
swerves mad
through the dying slack
of sun

he asks me how i like it
in vermont

i say, well
it is pretty and green
and clean
in that southern drawl
i can't shake

as the rain picks up
he asks me
how long i've been
in town
& he makes
a sharp turn
down a narrow street
that i have walked down
to grab groceries
with my boyfriend
many times before

i tell him
only a few months
just moved to town with my boyfriend
he laughs
is he white or black?

i whip my head around so fast
that the tips of my braids
swipe the window glass
like his wiper blades

i say *white*
and he says *i knew it*

there really aren't any
black people around here

as though
the black girl
in his backseat
was not actually there
at all

enfamil

once a week, like clockwork
it arrives on my doorstep:
a package of baby formula
i did not order.
the sender as unknown to me
as the intent. childless,
i reach out to my friends
with new babies—
perhaps there's been some mistake
i say
did you accidentally send me a package?

one by one, they text me back,
remarking with a dark humor
how they hadn't sent me a thing
& my horror,
newly implanted, grows
like the trail of ants
around a dead bird
on a sidewalk.

i am suddenly rosemary
without the baby,
as some person
who knows where i live
is convinced
that a child
should live there too.

days later, i think of this again,
as another friend
writes to our group about a miscarriage
she recently suffered:
they call it a chemical pregnancy
she blurts across our screens.

who knew that losing a baby
could be described
as clinical and sterile, as *chemical,*
like some scientific experiment
that just happened
to go wrong—
some cruel hypothesis
unrealized

that evening,
i examine the latest formula box,
the words it reads
in a certain unmistakable
tiffany blue:
Here's our first gift for the
Most Important Person in the World
& i do think it a small gift
& important too,
that i received the boxes
that were meant
for her

dear editors

would you like me
to tell you
about black pain

if you want
i can show you
my father's
my mother's
my baby brother's
my dead brother's
too

& it's certain now
as it has ever been
the permanency of death
the color of it
too

the mark it leaves
like ashes
on our foreheads

editors
i must tell you
i know there are secrets
you wish
to pry
from my mind

but i must tell you
i've locked them away
in the same
cold place
you've stowed
your hearts
for safekeeping

on housesitting for seven days

for major & didi

i walked in breathless. i shut the wooden door. i feared
the dark. i slept until i woke. i let the dog out. i let the
dog in. i followed the cat down the gravel path. i sat at
the kitchen table. i worked from home. i mined books
from the shelves. i carried them to bed. i lifted my left
breast in the bathroom mirror. i sat on the balcony. i
saw a stone face in the wood. i latched the door chain. i
heard the wind sift through the trees. i turned the heat
up. i slipped on your sandals. i picked up the packages.
i fussed with the cat. i filled out the medical intake
form. i opened the curtains to sunlight. i wished for the
rain. i threw on your favorite sweater. i smiled when i
touched your suede jacket. i thought myself important
in your office. i drank wine on your sofa. i imagined
you laughing. i cried in your shower. i blamed my
body. i envied your bed. i called for the cat in the dark.
i swallowed your aspirin. i peeked into your room. i
pulled the covers away from my lover. i rode into town.
i bought a book from the shop. i called you up on the
phone. i curled up until the pressure stopped. i waited
for the lights to come back on. i contemplated the
masks on the wall. i climbed the wooden stairs. i baked
a slab of salmon. i stole a dollop of yogurt. i wanted the
pills to kick in. i wondered how you two met. i should
have called my mother. i called my father instead. i
forgot my mask at home. i stuffed the trash into the

bin. i followed the dog into your office. i lost all phone service. i poured the french press. i counted your spices. i walked past *the sound and the fury*. i picked at my fro. i touched your picture frames. i fantasized about your telescope. i waited outside in the cold morning. i saw a leaf shed its green. i prayed as my lover slept. i touched the lump again. i cried in the shower. i jumped when the cat scratched at the door. i envied your bed. i slept too late. i stayed up all night. i remembered dreams. i cursed when the justice died. i walked around the cemetery. i saw my name there in stone. i searched for *the absurd man*. i sang as i lifted the sheets. i found moon jars in the night sky. i danced in your kitchen. i let the cat climb into my lap. i waited for the morning sun. i found answers in your books. i pulled out of the driveway. i counted to ten. amen.

re: the white woman who grabbed me in goodwill last week

the audacity
of her touch
reaching out
a pallid hand
from behind
a peeling gray
basket

i pulled
summer shorts
down from a rack
as she gripped
my shoulder

so hard
that i thought
i might have stolen
something &
somehow forgotten

then,
she finally spoke & said:
i just had to stop you
because you're beautiful

so beautiful
that she reached out
to pull me back through time

so beautiful
she had
to hurt me

* * *

i said
thank you
although
my shoulder stung

after all,
i have always been gracious
for pain

now
i'm sore & haunted
by the scream
of my own silence

* * *

when i told my mama
she just sighed
and said
skye, you need to pray

but i don't know
if she meant
for me
or for her

i pray
next time
she keeps the pull
of my beauty
to herself

avoid your heroes / trust me

for faye dunaway

i remember her
when i was fifteen
in a darkened classroom

my gray catholic schoolgirl skirt
still hung just below
my knees

her face curved
all elevated rapture
inside a bulbous tv
on wheels

in *bonnie & clyde*
blonde & beret'd
she swayed
in a depression-era cream slip
& a stolen car
as she hopped in with her boyfriend
& left her elderly mother behind

for navajo blankets & lovemaking
in fields of tall weeds & wildflowers
as the camera panned out

until i met her

years later,
biding my time in beverly hills
just a lingerie salesgirl at saks
when i climbed atop
a wooden ladder
& pulled down
a pair of sheer pale stockings
because she could not reach them

she was seventy-six then
& called me diana
living just to forget
my name

yet i still helped

until the day she came in
hunting for new sleepwear

i remembered
who she had been:
southern girl aflame
the one who taught me:
it is good to escape

so when she screamed
at me to shut up
after i said
pink pajamas
would look best
against her skin,
i silently blamed her age

& still i helped
even as she forced me
into her dressing room

made me stand
nose to corner
like a petulant child
needing to be punished

that corner,
as cold as her thin veiny hands,
tugging the back
of my black velvet dress

the shrill of her voice
asking me to button
the pink nightshirt,
anyway

years later,
i hear tales of her madness
on broadway,
firings, slurs & lawsuits
filed

& i wonder
as she continues
her wild & ambitious decay
whether or not
she still thinks of me
when she wanders, lost
into saks

howling for help
across rows
of overpriced cotton panties
& tiny sugar baby playsuits
as she searches for yet another
faceless black diana

how to cleanse your ratchet chakras

the psychic instructs me:
the supplies you need
are as follows; she says,
epsom salt, vinegar, table salt,
baking soda, and rubbing alcohol

(alexis realizes we are out of baking soda—
text the psychic
see if we can use pancake mix instead—
skye! it's the same thing!)

pour one cup each
into your best friend's bathtub
because you have no other
place to go
soak for twenty-five minutes
(no soap though)

concentrate & meditate
focus your energy
rinse your body

post-soak, get a sample
of your bath water
label it with the day and time of your bath
and leave it on my doorstep

journal how you felt
before, during, & after

take your crystal
put it in the water with you

rub it all over your body
then place it back in the bag
and under your pillow
when you sleep

during the day
put it in your bra
close to your heart

take your candle
light it in a bowl
filled with one inch of water
once you've lit it
it must stay lit

the faster it burns, the better
slower is worse

wear white for the next three days

vacuum the carpet
sweep all the floors
sleep only on clean sheets,
my dear girl

(that will be $300
for this week's work
no worries—
you'll be cleansed
by the time
rent's due
on the first)

burning blue

on lundi gras morning, my mother lights up
in the kitchen, she hops up & down;

her phone clutched like a precious diamond
in her left hand.
my best friend's calling, she exclaims,
she remembered me—
& i smile
as i hurry away, fixated,
on my own preparations:
makeup to apply & costumes to prep for the day.

later, i am walking out
of the bathroom, pastel pink wig laid
& silver space boots slipped on.

my mother sits in her red leather rocking chair,
tilting slowly back & forth,
a dark bible beneath her hand
when she says:
did i tell you what cassie said today? she asked.
i say, *no,* tracking the trajectory of the parades
on my phone, grabbing my fanny pack
to race out of the door.

my mother's face softens
under the press of a newly familiar pain:
she wished me merry christmas &
a happy new year—to me & my family—
she couldn't recall your names.

& i pause
with one hand on the frame of the door,
wanting to comfort her
but feeling so unsure.

at least she remembered, i said,
that this is a special day
& maybe that's what's most important
my mother agrees
but she sounds tired—
the memory of who her best friend was,
the time they shared
burning blue in her mind
like a gas lit stove top flame

the way things should have been

i should be there with you right now
having raced through the ice
just to get home

with wine & a fish from the market
for us to sauté
in a canopy of cilantro & lemons

as you hug me hello
& the cold drops
from my shoulders
while a sade record,
is it a crime,
plays

today it occurred to me
that one day i'll have to
take care of you

so now i prepare
build my little home
shelves for our books
to touch each other,
& breathe (again),
& a bed, we can once again share

i know you never think about tomorrow
& certainly not yesterday

but i do
& i will
for you

i'll spin this nest, warm,
like the spider
who lives on my windowsill
& wait
& wait
& wait

when the half black man i'm in bed with calls my hair nappy

i can hear it so clearly again
the sizzle of my hair
straightened sharp to blade

and that chemical smell: *relaxer,*
thick white & deadly
stirred in a plastic cup

my nose burns
before it is even applied
to my roots

the stylist adjusts
her latex gloves
to protect her hands
from what she's about to smear
across my bare scalp

she sighs,
parting my budding curls
into quadrants

resigned, she whispers
into my ear, as though
this is something
to be hidden:
your hair is so thick

i see it all in that second
he turns his light-skinned
body away from me in bed
laughing

he says
you & *this*
nappy hair

hope i don't wake up
with any of your little
curls in my mouth

his thick cruelty
cold as butter
brings me back
down south

to the hot comb in my stylist's hands,
the tub of blue magic hair grease
on the bathroom counter,
always emptied

to the saturdays
wasted in salons
or the chemical burns,
each a pulsing scab,
round and hard
as blood-fed ticks
dotted across my scalp
hidden beneath glossy
straightened hair

i open my mouth to speak

(& want to say
to him
tell me again
how much
your white mother
loves you)

but instead
i say
my curls are beautiful
i love my hair

so quiet
that i can't even
convince myself
of it

but he's
already
fast asleep

grocery list for when my ex comes to visit

seltzers of all flavors
that green salsa he likes
avocados
wine (on tap)
spaghetti sauce
bubble bath
lavender epsom salt
pillar candles
whiskey for balcony hot toddies
condoms
black teddy
sheer lace stay-ups
various meats (he'll want steak)
coffee
bread
another mug
to finally place
next to mine
on the shelf
black beans
brown eggs
tissues
matches to start
a fire
neither of us
will know
what to do with
a gift for him: lucille clifton divination cards

(later in my kitchen
he will pull one card from the deck
it reads:
today we are possible)

exactly three beers
the strength to watch him walk
through the door
the acceptance if he chooses
to walk out of it again

& scissors

to cut
down my braids
when he flies out
on monday morning

the remote year: a gentrified duplex

—*after jericho brown*

i begin the new legal job, remotely
hoping to grow there

i train on the new job, remotely
boss says:
you're getting nowhere

my managers discuss me, remotely
over microsoft teams
they say:
skye is the worst, i swear

i suffer in the attic, remotely
covid webmd tells me how much time
i will need to sweat there

i don't need to sweat to be hot
i don't need to be hot to be mad

i sit at my computer, remotely
hoping the landslide of emails
eventually stops
somewhere

i reconcile with my ex, remotely
he asks me:
what's keeping you occupied
up there?

my best friend consoles me, remotely:
skye, you can't quit
it'll get better, i swear

my mama prays, always remotely
says:
skye, i can't wait
'til you get
the hell up outta there

at work, i dodge the estates of mlk jr. & elvis, remotely
though my boss
ignores my emails
he still yells:
skye, why wasn't i made aware?

HR says if i leave i get no severance
damn, i tell my therapist,
this is so unfair

i finally close the computer, remotely
hoping the good hell
ends there

the day after the school shooting, the morgue posts on indeed.com seeking an additional funeral assistant

part-time work only
though demand is increasing

seeking: someone
who can deal with the living
they need more care
than the dead

must be kind to children:
the deceased
& their visiting friends

remember, we need to build relationships
everyone can be a future customer
this is the price of modern violence
so hand a piece of dark chocolate
to every child you see

make them smile
their parents will remember that
if & when they need
to come back

always be willing to learn
remain stoic in the face of unimaginable grief

greet & escort
when they ask, why did _____ happen
just nod and say:
i'm so sorry for your loss today

give them a coffee
so they can hold
something hot in their hands

the ideal candidate for this position
should be nameless & faceless
just another blur in the crowd of mourners

they'll look back years from now
not remembering you
& honestly
that's what counts

try to blend in
wear all black

& keep the children's caskets closed:
remember kids under six
have thinner skin
& softer bones

you see,
the bullet holes
are getting harder
& harder to mask

though we'll fill them
with plaster & clay
to show our customers
we are more than up
to the delicate task today

on the day of my resignation

i see a white girl
wandering around a cemetery
trying to be cool

i think
why search for the dead
in the dark
when you can just find them
scrolling down your news feed?

my phone buzzes with a work email
i realize
emails are just less interesting
headstones
all names
no faces

the dead as white & populous
as my emails

i can't keep track of them all

i have only been back in new orleans
for two weeks

when i learn about the three children
that fell into the river + drowned
trying to save each other

when they found the girl in slaughter, la
rotting in twelve years of her own filth
under the watchful eyes of her parents

when six people were shot at a bar on magazine st.

when three children dragged a woman to death
    in mid-city
when the DA decided to try those three children
    as adults

when i sat in city park
sucking down crawfish
& strawberry mead
and my best friend asked me
why i took him back
but not if i was happy now

when i kept putting off quitting a job i hated

when the mayor sent out her condolences
when she did it again the next day
and the next

when i told my mama they needed
to put the parents of the rotting girl
under the jail

when the body
of one of the drowned children
washed up on the mississippi riverbank

when the three-year-old got shot on burgundy
when the mayor offered
more thoughts and prayers

when my best friend asked me over cocktails
at the hotel st. vincent:
skye why won't you just come home

and i ask myself:
skye why don't you just come home

    i hear myself telling her:
    i never left

    & now i don't know who to believe

the day i was born

my father does not remember
the day i was born
the events, i mean
questions that were asked of him
like when my mother's placenta
burst like a supernova
and the doctor asked him:
who would you like me to save?
your wife or your daughter?
after learning
that my parents weren't married
& that my father
had no say in the matter,
the doctor turned to my mother:
we may very well lose the baby, he said.
who would you like me to save?
you or your daughter?
my mother closed her eyes,
horrified her unborn child
might not survive
as i began to drown inside her,
like one of those children
lost in the dark of the river,
when she turned to the doctor and said:
we are both going to live
we are both going to live

we buried monty today

in a pet cemetery my daddy
found in mississippi

my brother brought a girl
none of us knew to the grave

i tugged at my coat
as they lowered the casket
(a black file box
from office depot)
into the ground

later my daddy would tell me
that the gravedigger remarked
why, i've never seen a dog casket
like this before!

i asked: did he mean that in a good or bad way?
my daddy said
he thought he meant
good
but he couldn't
be sure

my mama got mad
because daddy put rupert,
my favorite bear
that i'd caught some some drunken
mardi gras long ago,
in the box along with monty

then my brother made a speech
as the dirt was pitched
into the hole

he says *monty*
you were my best friend
we even smoked together
as his thick freeform dreads
blow in the wind

i think
no one can tell me
that black people aren't
sentimental

later as we pull out
of the cemetery
my mom says
ju
did you really smoke
with monty

he says *ya*
my mama sighs
and says
wow
he never told
your secret

libre

—after claudia rankine

while in key west for a writing residency, you meet a seventy-three-year-old white man. you're sitting outside of a dive bar composing poems for strangers on a manual typewriter when he takes a picture of you without asking. he asks if he can send it to you on facebook. you say sure.

a few days later, he sends you the picture & tells you it went viral in a key west facebook group that has not accepted you yet, although you applied for entry days ago. it will be anytime now, he tells you.

he asks if you are going to see the new editor of a premiere literary magazine's craft talk and reading at the college outside of town. you have planned to go for weeks now, so you say yes. he asks if you need a ride there. you are hesitant—but you do need a ride. the campus is too far to reach on your bike. he says, if you want, you can go to the readings together and he will treat you to dinner. for some reason you can't pinpoint, you feel uneasy but still say okay.

days later, you both go to the craft talk. everything seems fine. afterwards, you and the old white man go meet the editor for dinner and drinks before his reading starts. there is not much time, only about an hour before he is scheduled to read his poetry onstage. you and the editor are the only two black people at the table of five. you try to make the most of the time and fill the air with congratulations and small talk. the old white man speaks about affirmative action and how key west was never part of the confederacy. you wonder why he needs to speak of these things right now, in this moment. the editor leaves to prepare for his reading. all is well.

the old white man pays the tab and suddenly you are on the back of his scooter, passing by warm blue waves of water and an abandoned boat called *freedom* once manned by a group of cubans escaping to america.

the old white man breaks the silence. wow, he says. that guy was so nice. you agree & tell him that he was just named the first black editor of a top tier literary magazine. in their long history, they've never had a black editor. oh, that's nice, the old white man says, but he's not *black* black.

you feel like you've been hit in the stomach as your long thick twists whip around you in the breeze. excuse me, you say, tightening your grip on his shoulders and steadying yourself on the scooter. what is that supposed to mean? well, he says, clearing his throat and speaking as casually as though he were commenting on the weather, his diction is *very* good and he seems quite worldly.

you don't even know where to begin with this. so you say, he grew up in the netherlands. with a pit deepening in your stomach, you tell this white man that the editor has lived all over the world. nice, the old white man says again.

you are lost in your thoughts when you realize he is turning the scooter around. you are no longer headed to the reading—now you are going to some other place. you feel like the blonde teenager in that joyce carol oates story—don't know where you're going, don't know where you've been.

he stops the scooter by the boat you passed minutes ago, the one with *freedom* scrawled in white on the side. the sun is setting into the water. it is getting dark. you wonder why you cannot speak. i'd like to take a picture of you next to the boat, he says motioning towards it.

you can't swallow. but you hand him your phone. you stand next to the boat called *freedom*, the wooden pieces of the hull jutting out into the soft sand. he takes the picture. he takes several pictures. you do not smile. you are holding back something inside you. you want to say things but you cannot say things.

suddenly, you are back on the scooter, though you do not remember climbing on it. the old white man takes a deep long breath. he tells you that he loves your perfume, that you smell *so* good. in your head you say, it's called *libre*. to him, you say nothing.

(when the white girl in the bathroom at hadestown asks if i'm cosplaying as persephone)

for charles simic

i smile graciously &
say *i am*
not

but drenched in her purple mink
with green eyes &
bathroom dyed
red hair,
she'll never know

that in hell
i too have raised
a cup to my lips,
not knowing
if it was filled
with wine or blood

& drank anyway

i too have kept
Death's empty bed,
warm

lit a candle dying
on his nightstand

in fact,
i have loved
so many different
Deaths

98

in doorways
in churches
at the breath
of my father's
wrath

i have left
my mother,
crying

for darker men
& moods & ways
as the flowers
were swallowed
by decay

i have prayed
to see a sun
long since
abandoned

cast my eyes down
as fair eurydice polished
our endless rooms of silver
with her strawberry hair

& laughed
at the quiet reproach
of the night, still

sugar daddy sonnet tiara

i dreamt of you so long before we met:
a rich mystery man on a lush street
offering me the world for just a taste
of the dark sunsets & valley beneath
my dress. shy, at garden of eden, you
watched me dance with another man, grinding
on the hot roof top. *did you have some fun?*
you asked as you ordered me my first drink,
something pink in a cup: dirty shirley
sweet & cool on my lips; you watch me sip
as lightning flash cracks up the key west sky.
how strange you found me on a street corner,
counting my loose change outside a sex shop.
we head inside the bar as the rain falls.

the drunk rain calls. we fall into the bar.
you want to know everything about me.
so i tell you about my poetry,
this residency, the home waiting for
me in nyc. i'm thirty-two, free,
typing poems for strangers on key west streets,
rolling around town for just two more days.
you're just as lonely as a tuesday night.
to my surprise, you ask me for a poem
& to take care of me the next few days:
dinners, cocktails, adventures, whatever
you want. my cheeks burn. what will you get, though?
Why, just the pleasure of your company.
i think, hell yes, let this strange pact begin.

yes, hell is close when our strange plot thickens:
we go to the green parrot, my fave bar,
where a white man once tried to follow me,
ducked into shadows to watch me walk home.
my girl shout shamed him into retreating.
i can't be both black & girl in these streets.
i flirt with you so the bartender sees.
quickfast, we order two tequila shots.
you say we'll talk about your poem sunday,
tomorrow at dinner – it's a downer
& tonight you want to play, amazed that
the whole bar knows my name – honestly, same.
i'm the only black girl on this island.
suddenly, i blink & we're on the beach.

the night blinks & the beach whispers softly.
the full white moon so close, almost in reach.
i throw off my sandals & hike up my
dress, wade into the sea. saltwater
swallows my thighs. it's four a.m., sunday.
workshop in five hours & i haven't
even slept, watching you bereft in the dark
waves; night so quiet i can hear the sand
breathe. you tell me you've never had a night
like this, though you were married once before.
you ask to hold me as we float in deep.
i oblige to see your illusions rise,
that look in your eyes. this, you say, the best
night of your life & lead me to your room.

best night of your life led me to this room:
the pool outside your window, glowing blue
like a turquoise tomb. i tell you i need
to use the bathroom; you laugh & say *girl,*
just pee on me, as you sit on the bed.
i'll pee on you for three grand, nothing
less, i say, *you ready to write that check?*
you're silent. i smile. guess we've found our max.
i ask you for an uber. clearly, it's
time for me to go; sand stuck between my
toes. i leave, rushed, though you ask me to stay.
in the car ride back, the night flees, fades.
once home, i peel off my dress & shower.
i wash the night & you away, so quick.

the night washes me away; beds you quick.
next morning, the room spins. hangover thick.
my alarm throbbing like a bursting vein.
you text: *we still on for dinner tonight?*
pick whatever restaurant you want, so
i do. hours later, i slurp my cure:
decadent seafood soup. shrimp, clams, snapper,
divine. we discuss your poem as the wine is poured.
you conjure your sister, dead, at fourteen.
shot by your older brother's gun, beneath
your favorite tree: an accident that haunts
you still. you couldn't sleep for days, weeks, months.
only thirteen yourself, innocence lost.
i head back to my room to write your poem.

the poem, head thrown back, writes me in that room.
my mind swims with thoughts of your long-lost home,
the tears in your eyes as you told the tale.
the next morning, we meet for breakfast: crepes.
i read the poem i've typed for you aloud.
i call it "what trees remember" sending
you into a delicate spiral; *how*
did you do this, you ask. *tell my story?*
you sigh and we sip more mimosas, slow.
my flight's in three hours – i'm in no rush, though.
you drop me back home & ask me, *how much*
for the poem? so i give you a hug &
shrug it off. say *no worries* with a smile.
still, you slip me a benny for the flight.

i slip the benny into my pocket.
your text message lands fast like a rocket.
call me when you can; swear i'll wait for you
my group chat buzzes: *skye, what will you do?*
i'll settle back into nyc life, quiet.
set about knitting you into sonnets,
cook, clean, lean into my own slow riot.

Notes

Acknowledgments

Grateful acknowledgment is given to the following publications and their editors, teams, and readers for giving early drafts of these poems their first homes and their gracious support of the work:

Antenna Press—blackbirds singing in the dead, a faster grave, the little gray schnauzer

Bear Review—libre

Blue Montain Review—the way things should have been

Dead End Zine, Issue Three—grocery list for when my ex comes to visit

Green Mountains Review—dear editors, far too kind

Miracle Monocle—fever dream

New Orleans Poetry Anthology—i have only been back in new orleans for two weeks

Rattle—can we touch your hair?, spoon-rest mammies

Reed Magazine—which one

Red Hen Press—umbrella

RHINO—when the half black man i'm in bed with calls my hair nappy

Rigorous—blackbirds singing in the dead, the little gray schnauzer, questions, to comfort you

The London Magazine—the boys with dead mothers
  get better with time

The Night Heron Barks—an ode to the w paris

The Southern Review—the day after the school
  shooting, the morgue posts on indeed.com seeking
  an additional funeral assistant; re: the white
  woman who grabbed me in goodwill last week

Tilted House—i remember

Xavier Review—#medusawasblackyall, currency

* * *

I owe a great debt of thanks to Regalo Press for giving
this collection a home, my editor Caitlyn Limbaugh
for all her assistance in perfecting the manuscript and
to my agent, Jane Hamilton, who championed the
work and never ceased in her offering of support and
encouragement when I needed it most.

To my family: Mom, Dad, and my siblings: Julian
Jackson, Kirk Malone & Carlos Jackson, you all are
my constant source of artistic inspiration. I love
you all so much and would not be where I am today
without you.

I am also deeply grateful to the Key West Literary
Seminar, who gave me a blissfully uninterrupted
month to generate and edit many of the poems that
appear here.

I'd also like to thank Cave Canem & The Frost Place for giving me support and the necessary community to perfect these poems.

To my Cave Canem family: Reginald Harris, Samantha Maren, Chelsea Williams, Judith Osilé Ohikuare, Kailande Cassamajor, Susha Poet, Nicco Diaz, Ugochi Egonu, Feyisayo Aluko, Iman Carter, Tangie Mitchell, Mike Lyles, Dana Knowles & Mitchell Bradford III—You each inspire me so much. Thank you for your gifts and all that you bring to this world.

To Toi Derricotte & Jericho Brown: Thank you for showing me the world of poetry in all of its infinite and beautiful possibilities. I found my own voice by listening to yours. I appreciate your unending mentorship & kindness.

My unending gratitude to my social and writing communities in New Orleans, Vermont, New York and Los Angeles. I lived so many different lives with each of you. Thank you for your guidance and unending support of the work. I love you all. And if I'm not with you, please know that I'm always missing you.

To my first poetry teachers at the New Orleans Center for Creative Arts: Andy Young, Brad Richard, Lara Naughton, Pia Ehrhardt, Chuck Perkins. Thank you each for taking me beneath your wings and guiding me as I began my journey as a poet in this world. Your lessons and instruction have never left me.

To my professors at the University of New Orleans
Creative Writing Workshop: Carolyn Hembree,
Kay Murphy, John Gery, Niyi Osundare & Richard
Goodman—Thank you for nurturing my voice,
expanding my knowledge and for your integral input
on the poems that appear here.

To my UNO CWW cohort: Carmin Wong, Swiss
McCall, Isaac Lauritsen, & C.A. Munn, I couldn't
have asked for a better group to grow alongside.
Thank you for always being there.

To all my classmates at the UNO CWW: I wouldn't
have been able to do any of this without you. Thank
you for giving me guidance, help and endless support
that I didn't even know I needed… & tears, along
with enormous gratitude, as I write these words.

To Ellis Anderson: Thank you for always encouraging
me to put my best writing out into this world. I have
accomplished so much because you believed in me.

To my therapist, Jay Terrill: Thank you for always
being one call away and for never judging me or my
experiences in this world. You were right after all: I
am exactly where I'm supposed to be.

To those that took the time to read and critique this
manuscript: Marissa Davis, Joan Kwon Glass, &
Christopher Romaguera, thank you so much. Your
feedback was integral to the formulation of this book.

To my workshop group: Rayon Lennon & Edythe Rodriguez, thank you for helping to make these poems into everything they came to be. I've been so honored to write alongside you.

To my lifelong friends, best known by the groupchat name, Vicious & Delicious: Christina Hunter, Alexis Gentry, Jonté Ray, Alexa Triplett, Daniel Toro & Sam Wheelock. I am who I am because you put up with me for all of these years. Love you all so much.

To Semaj Crumpton: Thank you for always being there with wise words and a calm presence. You have become like a sister to me. So grateful for you.

To Reda Wigle: Thank you for helping me through the madness of life and writing. You're always there to talk me into an adventure & out of sadness. You are such a light.

To Ben: Thank you for the love, laughter and adventures we have shared. And for always being willing to look after my heart and at my poems.

And my thanks to you, dear reader, for supporting poetry and poets. Thank you for trusting my work with your time and your mind. It means more than you will ever know. I do all of this for you.

Yours,

Skye

About the Author

Skye Jackson is an award-winning writer and editor from New Orleans, LA, whose poetry has appeared in *The Southern Review*, *Rattle*, *Green Mountains Review*, and was hand selected by Billy Collins for inclusion in the Library of Congress *Poetry 180 Project*. In 2023, she was a finalist for the *Iowa Review* Poetry Award. She currently teaches at Xavier University.